THE STUDS OF McDONALD COUNTY

Poems by Joan Yeagley

BkMk PRESS-UMKC
College of Arts & Sciences

University of Missouri-Kansas City
5216 Rockhill Rd., Rm. 204
Kansas City, MO 64110-2499

A Target Poetry Series Book

Acknowledgement is made to the following publications, books, and anthologies in which some of these poems have appeared: **The Kansas City Star, The Poetry Bag, Best Friends, Akwasasne Notes, Review La Booche, Poetry Now, The Little Balkan Review, University of Portland Review, Focus-/Midwest, Midwest Arts and Literature;** "The Blue Hole" **Four Bookmark Poets**, BkMk Press, Kansas City, Missouri; **The Missouri Poets**, Eads Bridge Press, St. Louis University, St. Louis, Missouri; **Kansas City Out Loud**, BkMk Press, Johnson County Library, Shawnee Mission, Kansas; **Above the Thunder**, Kansas City Association of Mental Health; **Voices from the Interior: Poets of Missouri**, BkMk Press, University of Missouri at Kansas City; **In The Middle: Midwestern Women Poets**, BkMk Press, UMKC.

Typography by Michael Annis
Cover illustration by Syd Baker
Printing by Walsworth (Marceline, MO)

Library of Congress Cataloging-in-Publication Data
Yeagley, Joan
The Studs of McDonald County

(A Target Midwest Book)
I. Title   II. Series

PS3575.E38S7   1987   811'.54   87-070659
ISBN 0933532-61-X

missouri arts council

Financial assistance for this project has been been provided by the Missouri Arts Council, a state agency.

BkMk Press—UMKC

Dan Jaffe, Editor-in-Chief
Pat Huyett, Associate Editor

*To the memory of my parents for their boundless love,
and to Hac: This boat needed a strong rudder.*

JOAN YEAGLEY married Hac Yeagley in 1951. They have four children, and three grandchildren. She organized libraries on the Pottawatomi, Kickapoo, Iowa, Sac, and Fox reservations in Kansas, established Job Information Services in system libraries, Library services for the Aged, and the Invitation Series which brought to rural libraries and community schools in the twelve county area programs dealing with aspects of the arts including painting, sculpture, drama, music, ecology, photography, dance, and poetry. She was twice a winner of the Kansas City Star Award for poetry. She has taught at Missouri Southern State College and now teaches Creative Writing at Crowder College, Neosho, Missouri. She has been a faculty member for the Mark Twain Creative Writing Workshop, UMKC, the Longboat Key Writers Conference in Florida, and the Missouri Valley Writers Conference. The Yeagleys live in an A-frame house they built for themselves on a limestone bluff overlooking Big Sugar Creek in McDonald County, Missouri.

CONTENTS

THE STUDS OF McDONALD COUNTY

The Studs of McDonald County

Summer boys down from haying,
Wheeze red dust,
Spit the raw stink of mown grass
And take the beach,
Capsizing with obscenities
A gentle generation of grandmothers
Porked in their inner-tubes.
Unzipping with the cheek of young Zeus,
They peel marble white legs of its skin of jeans,
Stow boots in the crotch of a tree.
Male grace
In the bronze loop of neck, shoulder, arm;
Civil War in the thigh;
They plunge.
From their beachhead on the granite buttes,
They pepper the girls with propositions,
Woo them with breakneck leaps
Then strafe the beach with insults.
The girls are cooler,
Will marry them down
And live in Carthage or Joplin.

Blackberry Summer

They are always ready before we are,
About the third week in July
When it's 98
And the humidity is the same.
The fruit swells,
Cascades, clusters of
Jewels big as my thumb.
I wonder the poor don't eat—
But there are different kinds of hunger.
With a gallon tin can
Swinging on its bail,
I pad down cloistered silence
Forest sealed,
Of dusty, one lane roads.
This is a solitary occupation—
Only gold-green beetles buzzing.
Besides sun-stroke, chiggers,
Snakes coiled
In the shade under all.
One must love thorns.
Not many have a talent for it.

Hootenanny Saturday Night

I

Like roots dug in the dark of the moon,
Hankerin's go deep.
Sooner believe the goose-bone prophets
Than KGLC's weather report.
Tuckin' shirt tails into jeans
A history survives
As coarse as linsey-woolsey
And as tightly woven.

II

Work songs measure
The rack, ripple, drag
Of muscle under a mule's hide,
The meter of a man's need
Steppin' off his land,
The plough scratchin' a long red itch.

And a one-armed farmer—
He's a fiddlin' fool!
Grips the bow with his knees
And works the fiddle against the horse hairs
As cats,
Fit with catnip,
Goose themselves up the trunks of trees.

Violet Dobbs and the Wanda Girls,
Aprons ironed stiff
As a backwoods sermon,
Dish up hot berry pies,
Coffee,
Jesus comin' "In the Sweet Bye and Bye."

Low, long,
Like the ache in the belly of the bass guitar,
A hillman sings his woman gone.

And violins can yelp, run,
Like hounds under a wolvin' moon
As old men fiddle older tunes,
Variations on a wind theme
That fools around these hills.

III

Walking to our car in the dark,
Kids skid and cut between us,
Between pick-ups stopped on the grass.
From the open school house windows
A music fills this Missouri night
As sunlight fills the moon,
Like David's harp
Struck
In the marrow of our bones.

Hank Williams Done It This Way

For Delmer Dale Cook

Heard the other day
Jean Goff's takin' lead guitar lessons up to Granby.
Seems like her and
Tony Gumm an' ol' Dolph Hicks,
Manville Williams, Nadene and Max Link
Are going to get the hootenannys up again
On Big Sugar Saturday nights.
Don't know where they'll git a fiddler,
You was the onliest one in all McDonald
Could really pull a string.
Leastwise 'fore your hands got so swoll
You couldn't finger.
But even then, Hoss,
You sure could pick that gi'tar.

They laid you out real nice.
There was three preachers.
Your cousin Gilbert's gospel group sang
And the Henson's sent a guitar of yellow mums.
Made us all feel better
Like them little fancy runs you done on
"I'm So Lonesome I Could Cry."

Angus Run

First, morning,
Then sun cuts at granite walls
And columbine drips from cracks like lava,
Brazing the dishpan flanks of the herd.
Angus,
Hides struck blue as cannon,
Amble the dry creek bed
Which lies exposed as a vultured bone.
Their tons erupt the stones
That echo a dry speech in hieroglyph
Of frond, mollusk,
Of notochord sarcophagused in pink lime.

Smelling the high grass,
Their meat surges like the river,
Swells the bank,
And moves the earthskin breasting the bones of the hills.

Cousined with cattle, but wise to ourselves,
Warmth grasps our skins
And touch ravels
A river of nerves to its damp source:
Awash in the spine of a perch.

The Shrink Says

I learned good scotch
Like I learned good men;
Belly laughs when the punch line
Drops decorum
With a ribald poke;
Straight from the shoulder stuff
Like a fast horse under my heels
Or the sure sense in my right shoulder
When bullets spin a beer can
Floating by, spink, spink, again, spink.

Trying, he says,
To be a father's need,
Son,
Wish of himself.

The Shrink says—

But no tad this—
Out at the elbows with herself—

Her mother's child
Loves a good man, a good drink, a good shot.

Fishing's Not Bad, Wish You Were Here

For D.D.

Luck being what it is, Smith,
I wish you more scotch than water.

Sun's up.
Headman says,
It   will   come   up   tomorrow!

But watch him!
                    Last week he did his rain thing,
And look what happened.

Stand up wind,
In the cattails,
On one leg,
Like a heron.
Catch less shit that way.
Beak: sixteen inches of nerve.

Write!
                    For the good times,
                                        Jones

15

Fire On The Hill

I

The smoke is yellow, then white
but there's no wind and all
afternoon the pall hangs,
builds. Come evening,
it purples like a bruise.

I'd like to think the sun
dropped like some great,
tired bear, shouldered a nest
for itself among the dry
leaves and sparked the ridge.

This was deliberate.

At first, no more than the
lavender tendril that wraps
a handful of withered grass,
barely brushes the brittle
brome. One flicker,
a dead cedar flashes,
the understory booms.

The fire creates a suction,
sends a pillar of heat
roaring into treetops,
a cornucopia of red rain.
Sap boils, trunks split, crack
like rifle shot, then crash.

II

I check wind direction.
Smoke insinuates
the corners of the house.
Nights, I watch the fire-line
move, inching, humping,
an orange palate licking
the hard edge of night.

Four miles west,
the rangers build a back-fire,
hoping the cliffs downwind,
to the east, will hold,
keep it from breaching the river.

Rain falls the third night,
cleansing as prayer or tears,
the end of this affair.

IV

Sunday I climb the ridge,
foot-loose, no paths anymore.
My license is my going.

Beneath my feet the spongy
tuft of leaf-mold's gone,
exposing fossil rocks,
a sediment spread by
a million years of death
on some empty sea-floor.
This globe's a pile of bones.

Downed trees smoulder, the ground's
still hot against my palms
and steam rises, hisses.
Drizzle alloyed with smoke
subdues a sun, cast
aside like a tarnished
Roman coin, of no use.

On the lee side of an oak,
an unburned hummock of grass.
I sit, my back against
the tree. A single bird
twits. No answer yet.

III

An early hawk rises
on silence in the pre-dawn
chill. Only the steady
chunck, chunck, as I
load and stack firewood.
A chicadee perches
near my shoulder, scolds
as I fill the feeder.
The first slashes of sun
strike the river below
and mist gathers, curls
on its surface. But my
mouth is full of ashes.

When Cold Gathers The Woods Close

When cold gathers the woods close,
I look for the wanton signs.
Of bittersweet shinnying up tree trunks,
Vaulting fences, or
Leap-frogging boulders.
It's like walking these same woods,
My arms crushing June poppies.
Each berry a sunburst,
Hot through my skin
Like a girl's blush.
Winter comes:
This color draws from me a smile,
Warms the ends of my fingers.

Persimmons

I

No use looking for bluebirds!
Time's not for it.

Our hollow roosts between ridges
Like a small brown bird,
Feathers wimpled.
Bare oaks wrestle with a light wind.
Sound has bled back
Like sap into the privates of the earth—
Only the shallow chuckle of the Sugar going on.

II

Balls! It's cold!
We camp in the open
Practicing for warmer deaths.

III

Persimmons hang
Ruddy on naked trees.
Offerings
For some jealous god.
Come on, Adam,
Load our laps
With gummy fruit!
Good— See—
They taste like dates.
Spit the seeds out. Make another season.
Knowing's good
And knowing that we know
Is better.

Baptist Primitive — A Christmas Poem

Whenever I pass the house out on 76,
I slow down to read the sign
Old man Croft nailed up on top of his roof.
It's big as signs that say, "Cafe," or "Eats."
But I'm in a hurry
And goose the pick-up up to 50,
As fast as I dare go around the curves
In the dry snow.

In Anderson,
I mail the kid's present
And buy Chinese Checkers for Charlene's kids.
I loved Chinese Checkers.
Wonder what the marbles will sound like
Going up the hose of Charlene's vacuum sweeper?
The clerk says, "Shall I wrap it? It's free!"

The one-way Main street is a funnel
For the blowing snow I stand against
Waiting for the jam on the street to move,
Cars backing into the street from both sides,
Each blocking each
And the predictable honker.
A rancher in a fleece-lined jean jacket
Pulls a new red wagon
Piled with gift-wrapped packages
Out the door of Tatum's
And loads them in the bed of his truck.
The bed is already full of packages.
The magnetic sign on the truck door says,
Bull Bedrick — Fence Building.
I see Bull cutting cross-country over gravel roads,
Riding the wind in his red pick-up,
Gift-wrapped packages falling off behind
Beside the mailboxes
Of this hill farm or that one.

Heading home,
The draft the truck makes
Sucks the snow under then over the fenders and hood.
This time I read Croft's sign,
"Beware!   Just a little further down the road
you are going to meet Jesus Christ.   For He is coming!"
Thick smoke spills over the rim of the short brick chimney
And there are three chord of firewood
Split and stacked in the yard.

I don't believe in Hell
But in sudden Epiphany
As three red birds
Fly out of the cedars.

The Taste of Wild Onions

Pick poke in the morning
While dew soaks shoe tops, pant legs.
Take only tender tips that taste like asparagus
And pickled last a winter.
For an abandoned homestead offer forty dollars.
He'll throw in blackberry brambles choking pasture grass.
Remember burns.
      Spring means huckleberries, wild strawberries
Fruiting the scars and dewberries creep beside cuts
Made by county road crews after winter's waste.
Forget north, east, south, west,
Rather, walk fence rows, logging roads,
Mastering the lay of the land,
Mapping springs, bee trees.
You need to know, first and last, where you are;
That sudden summer storms will pass, then turn back on you;
That new potatoes go three-fifty a hundred.
Take whatever work is offered.
Your neighbor will pay what he can
And his wife has more eggs than she can use.
In August, look for choke cherries, sand plums,
See how possum grapes arbor elms — a pruning hook is
helpful.
All white flesh from the river is sweet:
Bass, frog-legs, crawdad tails.
Simmer turtle for soup with wild onions.
When you spot a Hazelnut, mark it!
Squirrels have longer memories than men.
Hunt in November, killing what you need:
For stew two squirrels; for pan frying
three bob-white, two doves, or one rabbit.
Plenty is having enough to give away.
Come Christmas,
It may be hard to remember why you came;
A crisis, hardship, simply a need to get away?
Wandering these hills will teach you how to stay,
If you choose.
Buy good whiskey, ask the neighbors in.
Home is a choice, not an accident.

Spring on the River

After sharp winds
A softness.

On the gravel bar across the river
A Great Blue Heron
Opens his wings.
His mate stretches her elegant neck.
They bow.
She opens her wings.
Plumes rise on his head.
They circle to a primal strain.

A foot above my head
The Hummingbird fans his tail,
Flies side to side
In a delirious arc.

My bones dance
And I would make my nest
In the palm of your hand.

SWIMMING IN THE POND
AT HOMEWORTH

Swimming In the Pond at Homeworth

Like the osprey,
Getting to the bottom of things,
I circle this languid room,
Snaking between reeds, plantain,
And touch the roots of starwort.
My arms go water-witching for deeper space,
Where light rays waver like watered silk,
Settle like silt over the backs of twitching bass.
I fall headlong,
Shatter the lens of the world
From the outside in.

Perspicuity

The adolescent had a talent for drawing.
When she couldn't find the four letter word
In *Webster's Unabridged*
In fifth hour study hall,
She penciled figures on a beach,
The man mounting the woman
From behind
As dogs in the back yard,
Monkeys in the zoo.
She didn't know that
Trust turns lovers face to face.

Now, I smile, when our Great Aunt Bessie,
Tribal Mother of us all at eighty-two,
Leans across the quilting frame,
Winks,
And confides,
"I don't hardly ever have no fantasies no more!"

Fables Run To Roses

For our first anniversary,
The birth of each of our four children,
You praised me
With long stemmed roses.

I awoke in rooms flooded with fragrance.

Slicing an inch from each stem,
Dosing them with aspirin,
I tore my finger on a thorn.

Blood came
Velvet as blooms:
The extravagant pain of your metaphor.

Some dawns,
Memory tricks the brain.
Our bed floats on the flood.

Make a rose of your mouth.
Your tongue is a thorn.

The Visiting Poet Proposes Something

Like the moon's penumbra
This frieze of soul
Revolves from the warp
Of public sun:
Intaglio scotched
With intimate craters
And distressed gorges.

Carver of poems,
Your chisel's set for stone.
Skill that voices marble
Wants an eye for the jewel's heat.

Its just that dying's long
That souls chance it;
That love jumps
Like a virgin birth,
Tighter than the coital fist,
From the terror of stone;
That we believe this camaraderie
Of younger poets and older scotch:
This common heart's
Enough.

Emerson Said It
"All mankind loves a lover"

Compulsive Cleo,
All lemon in candlelight,
Anathema of backyard barbecues,
Swizzles martinis,
Bastes the hens,
While wives choose snakes under the roses.

Poor Tristan,
Had to resign from the club.

Abelard, painlessly emasculated
By the Chairman of the Board,
Mounts the Vice-president's chair.
His Heloise.
Marvelous in P.T.A. and pink,
Wistfully covets the cloister's joys.

All the world's Delilahs
Have blunted their shears,
And Mark has filed in New York State;
Isolde romps on Gretna Green,
Effervescent as steaming milk
Stabbing the bucket
Between a farm boy's knees,
While Sampson
Shakes his mane
And roars.

From an ad in *The Farm and Dairy*
Salem, Ohio

AUCTION:

Hartville Community Hall, 10:00 A.M. Saturday
The Estate of Miss Mabel Cabell
Lunch served at noon.

Mabel's goods are up for sale:
Decades deeded into light,
Offhanded, careless of their color,
Like flowers plumped with noon.
Memorabilia cluster like
Chrysanthemums, warming the room.

People trawl the shores of the room,
Angling to corner the catch on sale,
Spinning goblets like spoons in the light,
Reeling in rainbows, netting the noon.
Catfish, hooked on show-boat color,
Lured into quick bids, pretend

The gaff isn't barbed, There's room
For a gesture, for a token sale.
Let her French clock recall the color
Of Limoges seen from the bridge, of high noon
Enameled in green and gold. Let
Keepsakes like petals souvenir the light.

Amelia

Kansas City, 1938

Summer thunder splinters my dream:
Light stutters, bleaches the wallpaper roses.
Like a pup,
I scat to Amelia's bed,
Muzzle brown breasts.

While Bill waxes the Packard,
Amelia leads me up rawboned treads,
The stairwell a crusty throat,
Hoarse from coal smoke and lilacs,
To her room.

Sucking horehound sticks
From Nanny across the hall,
I lie on the floor
Reading pages of the *Call*,
Spread instead of rugs over scrubbed wood.
On the back grate
A Chase and Sandborn can of bacon grease
Turns yellow as the liquid afternoon.

Later, in the park,
Amelia's folks picnic in the shade.

Shy as a lock-kneed colt,
I stand in a ring of children,
Toe the grass.
"Girl, can you run? At school I beats the boys!"
"I can beat you," I say.

Racing to the curb and back,
We sprawl in the shade,
Gasping between giggles.
She pats the blond fuzz on my flushed arms
While I study the mystery
Of each tiny braid

Plaited into another.

Our lips turn blue from grape soda pop.

The heat arches like tented elms
As we loll in the wading pool,
Dresses ballooning in our laps.

A Park Attendant,
Silver badge on his uniform,
Braid on his cap,
Aims a leather swagger stick at me,
"Get out!   You can't swim with them niggers!"
I come out of the water,
The wet dress clammy against my skin.

Amelia pulls me on her lap.
I hide my face in the curve of her neck.
"Growing up is hard, Baby,
Growing up is hard," she says.

Lora

Her husband, John, remembered
To the Adult Sunday School
Of Hickman Mills Christian Church,
As to how Lora and three cohorts
Descended like a Holy wind on Duffy's hovel,
Bathed and shaved the old sinner,
Cleaned his room, washed his clothes, dumped his gin,
And force fed him homemade chicken soup.

Lora amazed John,
And long before the ladies organized for it,
Lora had her rights,
From John and everyone else,
Even the terrorized Duffy:
A respect earned from childbed,
A life of plain, dull work,
A pioneer certitude.
God and Lora
Knew what was right.

I see her launching a shopping cart
Through the A & P parking lot,
A bunch of white pin-curls jutting on her forehead,
Another cluster wagging like a sheep's tail
At the nape of her neck,
Her back formal as an oak.
The shopping cart seemed an extension—
An appendage like her chin—
Of her will.

I heard that Lora died
And felt a tug,
As if the earth slipped a cog,
Shuddered on its axis:
The shock of knowing
That living,
From now on,
Means losing.

Downs Syndrome/Natal Map

Lines for my Godson, John

Grabbing Scorpio by the tail,
You are born to Cancer rising;
Shaking down the ashes
Of our souls for new fires.
Moon in Pisces:
Anguish supple as the whisper
As the fern uncurls.

As a river itself,
Designs the grace of its ways,
Lines name your palms
With settled channels;
And a whorl of chromosomes
Like novae,
A galaxy of genes,
Chart the temper of your universe.

At the font
I name you,
Covenant my day with yours,
Past our spanned stars.

The Teacher

I need you friend
Like a hair-shirt.
You rasp esteem,
Assurance disconcert.

Bristles of self-doubt
Scold nerves raw.
The fly in my unguent,
You are the flaw

In the easy design.
You shear
Wool from false sheep
With strict meter.

I've had enough.
Conceit's my privilege.
Aspiration
Is a thin ledge

But I'll stand on it
And this late probity
My self. I hold
My equity.

Come on! What's this?
You! Deign to offer
Crusts of praise?
Are you my presbyter?

A Saturday Funeral in Lyons, Kansas

For a Priest burying a Priest
Ed Hartronft and Jim Viggers

Sitting in a wing chair
He fiddles with his pipe,
Watches plumped clouds
Snag tops of oil derricks,
Smothering Kansas,
As the old mother shows her album around the room.

Vested, he drives behind the hired car.
The procession curbs
Like a caterpillar arranging its parts.
The sexton waits in the wings
In a straw with a Stetson roll.

The town's widows hover
Beside the grave,
Clustering for warmth
Like bees in a winter hive.
He commits the body,
Kneading the moist dirt
Between his fingers.

The widows linger
Mumbling kindnesses,
Until he rolls up the funeral grass.
The sexton,
In striped bib overalls,
Brings the shovel.
"No!" Jim says, "I'll finish it.
I need a shovel in my hand."

39

Tornado

Loosed from coiling braids
of a madwoman racked
on her windy bed, a strand writhes,
rears, stretches its boa
mouth, swallows the pond,
sucks bricks from its mortar,
snaps the ribs of the city.
Medusa's hollow moan:
the thickening thrill of stone.

"The Judgment of the Birds"

for Loren Eiseley

In the morning
The birds fall:
A silence of pigeons
Floating outward,
A pulse of white wings lifting light.
They own midnight alleys,
Manhattan's wilderness
Of chimney pots and spires,
As from the unlit pit of sleep
They rise, whirl,
Till the mind's lit with spinning.

Once, Rome roared, "Pompey!"
Creased the air
And the birds fell.

It is the "Judgment of the Birds,"
That my fingers flex along the sill.
I discover a feeling for air,
Allegiance to
The cities of wings.

Veterans Day In Joplin

At 8th and Joplin Avenue
A nasty wind whips
Huge, leathery sycamore leaves
Into a flume, a spiral,
A devil of dust,
Then dies.
The next gust sweeps them
With tattered news-sheets
Around the base of the flagpole
In front of Memorial Hall.
Above, the American flag
Beats a staccato, rhythmic, thump
As it tugs against its metal clasps.

An old man hooks his elbow
Around the pole,
His dough-boy tunic unbuttoned to the wind,
Cap set squarely.
No high school majorettes
Snap their thighs for him,
No bands lead out with boasting brass,
No synchopated snares,
Not one congressman's
on hand to make a speech.

He stands alone with the names
Embossed on brass plaques.

Psalm 22

"Eloi, Eloi, lama sabacthani!"

Elias come, our bones are out of joint,
our tendons slide in the blood like wet leather
and some damn fool breaks our legs.
Israel trusted: tell that to the six-million
who ate nails of flame
while Job dibbled their ashes for a sign.
Hell!!
I am Job's fist!
God is wrong
To trust the Word to flesh.
Yet,
Love is the taste of ashes,
and ashes are clean.
Do fear's baccili feed
on the flame's joy?
The Hind of Dawn
Praises what it knows.

From the Porches

Glare ripens windows,
Punctuates bits of bottle glass.
An obsessive sun whitens.
Mauve follows sunset's sermon.
Martins celebrate the sky,
Absolve the day of its undoing.
In the name of God
They cross the air.
Night slips overhead like a chasuble.
My feet bruise roses.

A Late Afternoon

Her namesake,
My daughter,
And I
Sat with my dying mother.

We held small hands,
Transparent skin stretched, fragile
As the tensile surface of still water,
Yet ardent.
In her eyes the cast of recognition,
A near smile.

Quietude settled on the room
Like the amber salute of late afternoon.

Her grip tightened.
She looked beyond us,
As she thrust
Toward a light we could not see.

I remember
The Pacific beach colonies
Along Big Sur.
All the cottages facing west,
All the windows reflecting boundless sea, sky, light.

THE KEEPER OF FIRE

Nish Nah Bah

(Native American)

Aunt Minnie Wahquahbuskuk
Cries all the time.

I need new glasses.

The B.I.A.* in Horton says,
This year's budget for glasses
Is all used up,
Maybe next year.

They spend most of the Washington money
Spraying marijuana that went to seed
When the government planted it in Kansas
During World War II as a substitute for hemp.

Sure, it's on Indian land
But leased by B.I.A. to white farmers
Who grow fat corn, big pigs,
While we get drunk,
Once a year,
On the lease money.

Do glasses cost that much?

We are Methodists
But our boards are bare.
A meal is fried potatoes
And a box of whiting for twelve people.
There aren't enough forks to go around.

We are Catholics.
Our girls still get pregnant—
No tall, young husbands to fend for them.
If we ask for Welfare
To feed the babies,
We must sign away our land rights.

We are Native American Church.
Is it not good to eat God?
Peyote is sweet!
God, you are medicine;
Take pity on me, medicine.
White law won't recognize
A marriage said by our Holy Man.

Topeka means,
A good place to dig potatoes.
But mostly,
We dig ditches.

Today, the tractor tears up
An old cemetery.
We told B.I.A. it was there.
Would we forget our grandfathers?
But there were no headstones.
That was not our way.
And they leased it out anyway.

My grandfather's bones groan
And his skull screams
Against the tractor blade.

Aunt Minnie Wahquahbuskuk says,
I don't understand.
I cannot see.
White dove, Jesus,
Where are you?
The hawk sings a bloody song.
The American Eagle
Eats the eyes of my children.

*B.I.A.—Bureau of Indian Affairs

The Osage

The dawn has told us
Who we are
For as long as we can remember.
The doors of our huts
Face the east,
The rising sun.
I kneel there,
Prostrate myself and pray
Till sun bathes my face,
Flows like oil, balm
Into my pores.
And from the dark place
Deep inside
Joy sings up
To greet the dazzle
Behind the screen of willow leaves.

The Water Carrier

I will make a song to the water.
I have a lover
And I am mad with joy.
We move towards each other
As spills from hidden springs
Seek the same river.

I set out from our village
With my clay jar
Knowing he will leave his work
And walk with me.

Today, the river strains with spring rain,
Fertile with the silt of our land,
Urgent with power
As a woman at the birthing post.

Swimming on the skin of her swollen belly
A blacksnake comes,
Driving his body
To the rhythms of his own drums,
His proud head high above the water.

Around his head
A heron looms, wheels,
Great blue wings parting sheaves of air.

These omens shake us.

I will make a song to the water.
He cuts poles for a roof.

Pottawatomi Drum Song

Drum is an old man, Drum,
Alone he will cry, Drum.

All things come together where you are:
The wisdom which is sky;
Giving earth below;
Eagle speaks in the West;
With the wing of the White Canada Snow Goose,
North wind cleans our land;
All the unborn are coming in the East
Behind the day-star;
And South wind blows on the pumpkin.

Your hand is in my heart, Drum,
Red is life, Drum,
Hum-ta-hey Hum-ping, Drum
It is a good day, Drum,
Drum, Dance, Drum,
Drum,
Drum.

Out On The Rez

Brother and his woman live
In a house warmed
By chunks of elm and yellow oak,
Sweating in the kitchen range.
A blanket hangs over the door
To hold the heat.

Brother reads by kerosene lamps
And acquires wisdom.

The plumbing freezes.
A slop bucket next to the stove
Does for raw garbage,
The two year old's pee.

He hauls his kids
Through Kansas drifts
To meet the school bus on the graveled county road.

The rattletrap Ford won't start
So Brother walks a mile to split wood for the widow,
Carries home a kettle of soup.
Of an evening, the men come by,
Sit in the kitchen and smoke,
Talk about layoffs,
Wonder when work will pick up.

Brother's woman fries bread,
Rolls it in sugar.

The Keeper Of Fire

My lover waits.
I catch his fleeting shadow
Behind and always on my left side
As one notices
The soft, throated dart of the quail.
He is beautiful
But I disdain his grace.
I was a proud woman
And not easily taken, nor surprised.
Once in a glade I met a doe
But the cast in its eye was strange.
I turned in time
As it reared to trample me.
His respect is great.
All these years I have kept the fire
And must be accorded the last privilege.
The women will tear away my rags,
Dress me in new clothes.
They will comb down this old white head.
My hair will fall to my waist,
Black, glossy as the upstart crow's.
I will dance.
All the others will fall away.
I alone will step to the right, making small feet,
Beat sticks, sing a tremolo,
Homage the Four Directions.
Only then, only then,
Shall I cover my head,
Taste the flame of his mouth.

OTHER BOOKS FROM BkMk PRESS

Tanks, short fiction by John Mort. "Chilling glimpses of the Vietnam War. These are terrifying, but sensitive stories." —*Bobbie Ann Mason.*
$8.95

Missouri Short Fiction, edited by Conger Beasley, Jr. Twenty-three short stories by Missouri writers including Bob Shacochis, Speer Morgan, James McKinley, John Mort, Charles Hammer, David Ray and others.
$8.95

Voices from the Interior, edited by Robert Stewart. Poems by over 50 of Missouri's finest poets.
$6.50

Modern Interiors, by Stephen Gosnell. Quality lithographic reproductions with short interrelated fictional pieces.
$12.95

Selected Poems of Mbembe Milton Smith. "One of our most nourishing poets... He used language deftly with lively, affectionate respect."
—*Gwendolyn Brooks.*
$8.95

Artificial Horizon, by Laurence Gonzales. "...a first rate young writer whose work merits attention from anyone seeking lively idiom, authentic detail and a fresh point of view..." —*Edward Abbey.*
$8.95

In the Middle: Midwestern Women Poets, edited by Sylvia Wheeler. Poems & essays by Lisel Mueller, Faye Kicknosway, Joan Yeagley, Diane Hueter, Sonia Gernes, Janet Beeler Shaw, Roberta Hill Whiteman, Dorothy Selz & Cary Waterman.
$9.50

Dark Fire, by Bruce Cutler. A book-length narrative poem, "...a lively, imaginative, and finely crafted tale of modern life." —*Judson Jerome in Writer's Digest.*
$6.25

Wild Bouquet, by Harry Martinson. The first American collection of these nature poems by the Swedish Nobel Laureate. Translated and with an introduction by William Jay Smith and Leif Sjöberg. $10.95 cloth

Writing in Winter, by Constance Scheerer. "...one of the fresher voices out of the Midwest...vivid and memorable." —*David Ray.*
$5.25

Hi-Fi & The False Bottom, by Goran Stefanovski. Two plays by a well-known Yugoslavian playwright, translated from the original Macedonian. Introduction by James McKinley.
$8.50

The Record-Breaking Heatwave, poems by Jeff Friedman. "This is urban poetry, working class poetry, strongly felt, carefully observed, cleanly written..." —*Donald Justice.*
$8.00 cloth

The Eye of the Ghost: Vietnam Poems by Bill Bauer. "Bill Bauer takes us well into the experience of Vietnam with a sure sense of the catastrophe that war proved for those who were involved. These poems demonstrate not only craft and dedication to the poet's art, but also an abiding commitment to justice and compassion." —*Bruce Cutler.*
$8.00 cloth